Asset Allocation Essentials

Simple Steps to Winning Portfolios

BY MICHAEL C. THOMSETT

FOREWORD BY
BLAINE MAXFIELD
SVP, SunGard Online Investment Systems

MARKETPLACE BOOKS
Columbia, MD

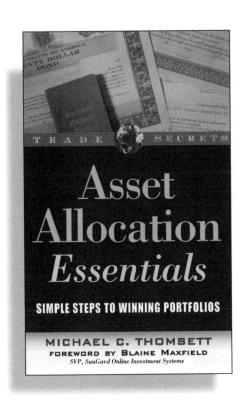

TRADE SECRETS

Asset Allocation *Essentials*

SIMPLE STEPS TO WINNING PORTFOLIOS

MICHAEL C. THOMSETT
FOREWORD BY BLAINE MAXFIELD
SVP, SunGard Online Investment Systems

Titles in the FP Books Trade Secrets Series

The Life Insurance Handbook
By Louis S. Shuntich, J.D., LL.M

Asset Allocation Essentials
Simple Steps to Winning Portfolios
By Michael C. Thomsett

The Long-Term Care Planning Guide
Practical Steps for Making Difficult Decisions
By Don Korn

Understanding ERISA
A Compact Guide to the Landmark Act
By Ken Ziesenheim

The purpose in going through the exercise of studying asset allocation is to ensure that goals and risk tolerance levels have been fully defined, and that investors and financial advisors alike can proceed on their journey knowing exactly where they are going.

—Michael C. Thomsett

This book, along with other books, are available at discounts that make it realistic to provide them as gifts to your customers, clients, and staff. For more information on these long-lasting, cost-effective premiums, please call John Boyer at (800) 272-2855 or you may email him at John@fpbooks.com

ISBN 1-59280-058-0

Printed in the United States of America.

1 2 3 4 5 6 7 8 9 0

Contents

Asset Allocation Essentials

Simple Steps to Winning Portfolios

Foreword

Since Harry Markowitz's pioneering book, *Portfolio Selection*, was published in the 1950s, asset allocation and Modern Portfolio Theory (MPT) have played an integral role in the construction of every investment portfolio. Roger Gibson later popularized the concept, presenting it in even more accessible terms in his landmark work, *Asset Allocation: Balancing Financial Risk*, currently in its third edition.

Now, this compact new guide by Michael Thomsett—a well-known authority and bestselling author—brings the concept into clear focus and puts it in the context of the contemporary investment world.

After experiencing the boom, bust, and bumpy markets of recent years, investors and advisors alike have learned firsthand the all-important role proper asset allocation plays in every portfolio. The corporate scandals that reinforce the ERISA requirements have further driven home the important role asset allocation plays in a portfolio—along with the sound decision-making process that is used to determine the appropriate asset allocation mix for each situation.

The use of portfolio optimization software to perform MPT calculations has grown with the interest in asset allocation and the changing investment climate. Formalized Asset Allocation Modeling began in the insurance industry many years ago, as actuaries with extensive mathematical training would calculate the impact of changes in interest rates on insurance company assets and liabilities. Banks performed similar internal asset/liability studies.

Then, in 1974, with passage of the historic Employee Retirement Income Security Act (ERISA), pension plan sponsors and other fiduciaries now had a *legal* requirement to document all their investment decisions. Pension funds were now bound by law to limit the investment risk in every fund to that taken by a "prudent man," prompting institutional funds to undertake formal diversification studies.

By the 1980s, the concept of asset allocation began to reach the retail investment industry. New formulas were developed to handle the complicated tax planning issues faced by individual investors. The brokerage industry was changing, ERISA continued to play a major role, and asset allocation was a concept that fit perfectly into the evolving investment industry paradigm.

At the same time, computer technology was becoming powerful enough to resolve many allocation and diversification issues easily on an advisor's desktop computer. While the first generation developers of asset allocation software were true "rocket scientists"—who created complicated programs for institutional investors that ran on big mainframe computers—the new PCs allowed the arcane principles of MPT to be accessible enough to the typical advisor managing portfolios for individual investors.

In 1990 Frontier Analytics, now an operating unit of SunGard Online Investment Systems introduced a PC-based asset allocation software for both retail and institutional investment advisors. Tens of thousands of investment advisors now use our software to prepare asset allocation analysis for millions of portfolios—and we continue to update, revise, and develop new applications that keep the software current and in tune with the needs of today's advisors and their clients.

We are always pleased to come across new material on asset allocation that provides a fresh approach and innovative strategies. Works written in non-intimidating language that time-crunched advisors can get through quickly, yet are simple enough to share with clients—are even more attractive.

Asset Allocation Essentials is just such a work. Divided into four parts, each section features one of the four key factors that are essential for constructing solid, asset-balanced portfolios. Chapter 1 presents diversification in all its many forms, followed by an overview of asset allocation risks. Chapter 3 outlines essentials for developing a personalized program suited to each individual's needs, and the book wraps up with a look at common misperceptions about asset allocation and core ingredients for creating a winning portfolio.

Thomsett's concise guide is a great primer. It's a quick-read refresher course and a handy way to get back to basics. It also makes great reading for clients who need a better understanding of the value that proper asset allocation plays in building a safe and profitable portfolio over time. And — it helps to reinforce the principles that are at the core of our own software products. I believe everyone — professional or individual investor — can learn something by investing some time reading this new guide.

Blaine Maxfield
SVP, *SunGard Online Investment Systems*

Introduction
WHY ALLOCATE?

To some investors, "asset allocation" is indistinguishable from diversification. While the two share some characteristics, they are not really the same.

The purpose of this book is to help the serious investor work with his or her financial advisor in developing intelligent strategies for the long term. While any portfolio certainly should be *diversified* among several different investments as a matter of practice, it is equally important to *allocate* a portion of total resources. That allocation is made between highly liquid investments (local savings accounts, cash on hand, and money market funds, for example); low-risk but less liquid investments (certificates of deposit, IRAs, for example); long-term and very illiquid investments (a home is the most obvious in this group); and growth investments earmarked for specific future needs (such as the stock of well-managed companies being saved for retirement, or long-term investment-grade bonds as savings for a child's college education).

Asset allocation contains the essential features of diversification. In fact, those features are the foundations of an asset allocation plan. However, in viewing the larger financial plan developed by the investor and the financial advisor, allocation takes on a more expanded role. Assets in all classifications should either be diversified or otherwise protected. (For example, when you open a savings account in an FDIC-insured institution, your money is protected already.) However, asset allocation has to be defined in its larger context: It is the process of determining how segments of available capital should be invested. This determination is based on (a) the amount of capital in a portfolio, (b) the knowledge and experience of the investor, (c) personal risk tolerance level, and (d) the specific objective of the plan and its segments.

To an extent, asset allocation may also be determined or altered based on ever-changing economic circumstances. The ability to anticipate and time such change is not a simple matter, and for most investors, the cyclical adjustments likely to be made within a portfolio are going to be determined on an individual basis rather than as part of a more complex economic analysis. For example, if you as an investor owns a particular stock and its fundamental attributes are beginning to change, you might conclude that its risk factors are on the rise; so you take your profits and invest in a stock more in line with your specific goals and risk tolerance. Or you own a bond whose investment grade rating has been downgraded; you may decide to replace that bond with another whose current value is comparable and whose nominal yield is the same, but whose safety rating is a grade higher.

These examples are typical of the kind of ongoing maintenance that every investor performs. The essential feature of asset allocation goes beyond diversification in the sense that it divides up a portfolio based on the needs, resources, and goals of the individual. The concept of allocation began many years ago in the insurance industry, but is now widely recognized as a technique that can be used just as effectively by individual investors. Insurance companies usually lose money each year on their premium business; the cost of commissions, overhead, and claims payments usually exceed premium income. However, well-managed insurance companies are also cash-heavy and they make annual profits on their investment portfolio. Insurance companies are among the largest institutional investors, and they buy a wide variety of stocks and bonds as well as real estate. Because a lot of capital is at risk, insurers developed the idea of asset allocation to ensure that their risk tolerance levels were diversified, and that they were not exposed to market surprises that could be disastrous.

The actuarial approach that insurance companies use to mitigate their risks is similar to the mortality risk analysis the same companies perform. By studying the likelihood of claims that are going to occur from one year to the next, the companies know how to set premium levels. When the ongoing cost of commissions plus general and administrative expenses are added in, the competitive company works on relatively thin margins. So a fairly sophisticated investment model is essential.

For individual investors, and the advisors who counsel them, the amount of capital in play is far less than the big insurance company portfolios. And as individuals, you have direct control over every portfolio, so there is no need for a complex system. In fact, the high-level mathematical modeling performed on the institutional level would be of little use to you as an individual. So the approach to the idea of asset allocation used in this book is practical, non-technical, and most important of all, applicable on the individual level. Asset allocation involves a series of strategies that can and should be incorporated into every financial plan, rather than a theoretical concept with no real relevance.

The process of asset allocation is an intrinsic part of the plan, but its development should be an outgrowth of common sense and a logical method for managing resources. You may think of allocation as an expanded, or more sophisticated, form of diversification. It is that—and more.

We all think of diversification as a way to prevent a single turn in the market from affecting an entire portfolio. Stock market investors have learned painful and expensive lessons about the importance of diversification in recent years, and every investor should remain vigilant about the various risks posed in any form of investment. However, asset allocation goes beyond the mere identification of different investment products or market sectors. It is the element that brings together your financial plan, by marrying risk tolerance to personal goals and objectives. Once a plan is coordinated in terms of asset allocation, you are on your way to creating and managing a well-developed portfolio, and a strategic approach that makes sense.

This book is divided into five chapters. Chapter 1 is involved with the importance of diversification in its many forms. Next we talk about asset allocation risks, followed by Chapter 3, the personalized program. In Chapter 4, we summarize common misconceptions. Finally, Chapter 5 presents questions and answers to review your knowledge. Remember the purpose in going through the exercise of studying asset allocation: to ensure that goals and risk tolerance levels have been fully defined, and that investors and financial advisors alike can proceed on their journey knowing exactly where they are going.

Chapter 1

THE IMPORTANCE OF DIVERSIFICATION

An effective program of asset allocation depends on a thorough understanding of *risk*. The proper management of risk is through diversification, the foundation of your asset allocation program. However, diversification often is not understood thoroughly.

In this section, diversification in its various forms will be explained. You will see that by managing your portfolio using diversification, you will be able to develop your allocation program. Most people think of diversification in terms of spreading exposure, or market risk. "Don't put all of your eggs in one basket" is the best known advice for those seeking to diversify; however, that is only one type of diversification. Many other, equally important methods for diversification should be kept in mind as well.

Forms of Diversification

Market risk is a starting point for developing a program of diversification. Remember, to most people, asset allocation is thought of in rather basic terms. For example, you may determine that you want to put 40% of your assets in stock, 40% in debt securities, and keep 20% in cash. This is a basic allocation of assets. The 40% in stocks may then be spread among several different stocks, achieving basic diversification.

This example typifies the common investment strategy and approach to portfolio management. It serves as a worthwhile standard model; however, it does not address other types of risks to which every investor is exposed, nor does it deal practically with (a) limitations of capital for those just beginning their long-term investment plan, or (b) the goals involved with investing in the first place, which should determine how resources are allocated.

For example, if you have recently used the majority of your savings for a down payment on your first home, then in practice, you are nearly 100% allocated in real estate. For analytical purposes, this is inaccurate. Real estate as an investment vehicle should be considered apart from your primary residence when analyzing how your portfolio is allocated. Even so, in your comprehensive financial plan, you should not ignore the importance of your home as an asset, probably your most important asset. So remember that the purpose of asset allocation is to distinguish one investing goal from another, not to merely apply some formula without underlying justification. If you read in the financial press that the common "wisdom" tells us to invest 75% in stocks, 15% in debt, and 10% in cash, remember this basic observation: This form of advice should be ignored. No one formula for allocation can possibly apply to each and every investor. Your goals and objectives, risk tolerance, and available resources are the determining elements in designing your risk allocation program (see Figure 1.1).

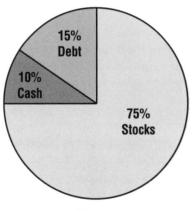

Figure 1.1
TYPICAL ASSET ALLOCATION PLAN

Let's examine the forms of diversification you need in order to manage risk in your portfolio. We divide these into five areas: Investment, market sector, product, risk factor, and investment goals and objectives. As shown in Figure 1.2, investment risk is broad by definition; market sector risk is less broad; and product risk is narrowly defined. The remaining two forms of diversification — by risk factor and by investment goals and objectives, are generalized and belong outside of the broad-to-narrow range. These distinctions are important because the type of risk has implications for every investor.

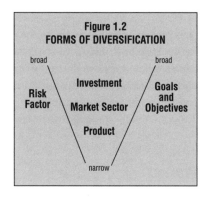

Figure 1.2
FORMS OF DIVERSIFICATION

Investment

Investment diversification is the broadest form. This means that you should invest some of your capital in different markets. You need to keep some amount of liquid investment, such as a savings account or even cash, readily available for emergencies. An emergency can mean anything from a needed auto repair on a three-day weekend to the loss of your job. So the level of your emergency reserve should be established for a range of contingencies. At the same time, you cannot anticipate all possible emergencies, nor can you always afford to keep enough money in liquid accounts. In our modern society, lines of credit have replaced the traditional emergency reserve fund.

Some level of capital may also be put into equity or debt. In their most common forms, equity means stocks and debt means bonds. These three together — cash, equity, and debt — form the basis for most investment-level diversification. More sophisticated or specialized investors may diversify further in speculative investments such as options or futures, or in tangibles like rare coins, metals, stamps, antiques and collectibles, and other very limited markets.

Market Sector

Market sector diversification is the second category. Concentrating for the moment on equity investments (stocks), it is important to identify the attributes of various market sectors. Some sectors are especially sensitive to interest rate changes and other economic and cyclical factors outside of the market. Many sectors depend upon trends in the labor market. Some others are subject to one-year cyclical change, such as the retail sector. When you are investing in different stocks, it does not make sense to put all of your capital into stocks that are subject to the same cyclical, economic, and market factors. You would not be well diversified if you purchased nothing for computer stocks, utility company stocks, or retail stocks, for example. You also need to diversify in terms of market sectors.

Product

Product diversification is a narrow form of diversification within a single market, such as the stock market. You can purchase stocks directly within the market. However, you may also diversify within equity markets. For example, you can place some of your equity capital in real estate investment trusts that are traded publicly, various types of mutual funds, or options. In all of these instances, you remain in an equity position but not all of your capital is invested in stocks. A variation on this theme involves the options market, where strategies can be employed for a broad range of purposes. These include hedging risk in other portfolio positions, augmenting profits by writing covered calls, simple speculation, and controlling a block of stock without putting all of your capital at risk (leverage through options). All of these strategies represent different forms of product diversification.

Risk Factor

Risk factor diversification is overlooked too often, but should be remembered by every individual investor. You are different from everyone else in terms of your risk tolerance level; so you need to design a specific level of risk that you find acceptable. For most people, this means defining a *range* of risks tied to product attributes (profit potential) as well as personal risk tolerance. The variation in risks between investments is significant, and some investors forget this important fact, concentrating instead on the potential profits alone. This is a mistake. Remember, profit potential is one side of the coin; the other side is risk exposure. The greater the profit potential, the greater the risk. This dynamic is inescapable.

Diversifying in terms of risk requires careful definition. You may believe, for example, that a particular investment is foolproof and that you are certain to make a profit. This occurs when emphasis is placed on profit alone, rather than on a careful analysis of the larger picture, meaning a review of risk/reward as a single factor. It is not realistic to define yourself singularly when discussing risk. For example, you might say, "I never speculate. I look for long-term growth and I am conservative." However, is that a complete enough definition? Perhaps that parameter is appropriate for the portion of capital being allocated for retirement or college education fund for children. At the same time, you may discover that other risk levels are appropriate for different investments.

For example, if you own your own home, your risks are far different than risks in the stock market. You live in your home, so you directly control its condition and value. You have homeowner's insurance, so you are protected against catastrophic loss. You know that historically, home prices increase over time, usually beating inflation. With all of these features, your home is certainly "safe" in comparison to the uncertainties of the stock market. Does that mean you should sell your stocks and invest in rental properties? Perhaps you should use your investment capital to accelerate your mortgage payment, reducing your debt.

> **Remember, profit potential is one side of the coin; the other side is risk exposure. The greater the profit potential, the greater the risk. This dynamic is inescapable.**

This example illustrates that awareness of risk factors is essential for allocating your capital appropriately. However, the need for diversification is apparent as well. It would not be wise to devote all of your resources in a single risk factor, so in your long-term portfolio you need to accept the reality—your real risk tolerance requires accepting different levels of risk, and diversifying accordingly.

Investment Goals and Objectives

Investment goals and objectives is the final defining factor for diversification. Every investor needs to use his or her goals and objectives as the ruling and defining factor in the important question: How much risk are you willing and able to tolerate? When you diversify in terms of your investment goals and objectives, you operate within a well-defined framework. Those goals and objectives dictate what investments are appropriate. For example, if one goal is to save up cash for a down payment on a house you want to buy in two years, it would not make sense to invest in assets that might not be available in that short time. If you are saving money for your child's college education, you know exactly when you will need those funds, so you will seek growth-oriented investments that will be available to cash out at the right time. If you are in your 20s or 30s you can afford to use higher-risk and aggressive growth products for your long-term retirement account; if you are in your 40s or 50s, you need to reposition your investments to preserve capital.

These examples demonstrate how goals and objectives specifically define the kinds of risks you can afford and, as a result, they require an important form of diversification. Too many investors begin their program by trying to identify a mode of diversification, and then fit their goals and objectives into that mode. Better planning requires that you begin by identifying your goals and objectives, selecting products appropriate to them, and then diversifying in accordance with the defined and required attributes (as well as time restrictions) for each goal.

Pitfalls of Diversification

We have established that diversification serves as the foundation for your program of asset allocation. Diversification is defined in several classifications and your personal goals and objectives dictate what forms of diversification are appropriate. The whole matter of designing your personal financial plan is integrated, dynamic, and volatile.

Your plan has to be *integrated* rather than segmented. It makes no sense to consider your goals and objectives, risk tolerance, appropriate levels of diversification, and specific product selections all in isolation; these are all parts of a singular process.

Your plan is *dynamic* rather than static. It has to change with changes in markets and products, your income and capital resources, family status, job and career, and personal development (changes in attitudes, leading to changes in personal goals). No plan remains constant throughout your lifetime. Consider, for example, how your goals have changed in the past 10 years. Your overall goals might be the same, but your attitudes towards investing and your risk tolerance have changed. No doubt, your income level and capital levels have changed as well.

Your plan also is *volatile* rather than safe. There are no foolproof plans, so you are going to be exposed to risk at some level no matter what you decide. Even keeping all of your money in cash in your mattress is a form of risk. Not only would it be vulnerable to loss through fire or theft, but inflation would gradually erode the spending power of your capital. At the very least, you need to develop a means for matching or beating inflation. Among the pitfalls connected to methods of diversification are too much/too little, the failure to monitor, failure to diversify, and timing problems. These are listed in Table 1.1.

| Table 1.1 |
| **PITFALLS OF DIVERSIFICATION** |

Too much or too little
- Inflation and taxes
- Over-diversifying
- Under-diversifying

Failure to monitor
- The need to review
- The importance of change

Failure to diversify
- Ensuring you are really diversified
- Avoid self-deception

Timing problems
- Market conditions matter
- Markets change

Pitfall #1: Too Much/Too Little Diversification

The first problem to overcome is *too much or too little* diversification. No one level of safety is appropriate in every case. You might be comfortable at the beginning of your personal financial plan design placing all equity portions of your portfolio into a mutual fund with a positive track record. However, as funds accumulate, it might be preferable to move funds into a dozen or less stocks, purchasing shares directly. In this example, you would move from a very broad level of product diversification (mutual fund) to a very narrow level (direct purchase). However, in the mutual fund, there would be a tendency for the entire portfolio to be designed with a single investment goal in mind (aggressive growth, for example). When you buy stocks directly, your fundamental analysis might end up with more diversification in terms of your personal goals and objectives.

In trying to identify the right level for diversification, one danger is that you could try to be so broadly diversified that you undermine its very purpose. Excessive diversification can create a situation in which advantages in one portfolio area are offset by disadvantages in another. Remember, profit is always accompanied by risk; and the greater the profit potential, the greater the level of risk. In the stock market, for example, the most volatile stocks are likely to pose opportunities for the greatest price movement, both up and down. So risk is an inherent feature of investing. If you diversify to the level that your portfolio is completely hedged against risk, you also cancel out the potential for making a profit.

Going in the other direction—not diversifying enough—is an entirely different problem, but far more common. "Don't put all your eggs in one basket" is a well-known piece of advice, but time and again, investors forget to follow it. So a fad comes along, like the late-90s dot/com industry. Investors put all of their capital into stocks of companies that have never reported a net profit (thus, there is no price/earnings ratio to compare and no valid fundamentals to monitor). Eventually, those investors lost all of their profits and, in many cases, much of their net worth. It makes the point that the "one basket" is a dangerous place to deposit all of "your eggs." A more balanced approach is demanded for a prudent, well-designed portfolio.

One factor in deciding how much diversification is required has to be the break-even point. Far too many investors never ask the question, "What return on my investment do I need to break even after taxes and inflation?" But this is the crucial issue you need to address to decide your minimal diversification and risk. Remember, you cannot just fail to invest because inflation will create an annual loss of spending power; and when you do invest, some portion of your investment profits are taxed. So inflation and taxes present a double hit on your net profits.

To compute your break-even point, divide your assumed rate of inflation by your percentage of after-tax income. For example, let's assume that you believe that your annual inflation rate is 2% (the rate at which your capital will experience less spending power). Let's also assume that you pay a combined federal and state tax rate of 31% (the tax bracket, or the taxes levied against your taxable income). The after-tax income in this case is 69% (100 less 31).

To compute your break-even rate, divide the inflation rate by your after-tax income percentage:

$$\frac{2}{(100-31)} = 2.9\%$$

In this example, you need to earn an overall net profit of 2.9% from your investments. If your net profit is lower than this level, you are losing money, and you will need to examine how you need to

	Figure 1.3 BREAK-EVEN RETURN ON INVESTMENT			
Tax Rate	Assumed Rate of Inflation			
	2	3	4	5
22	2.6%	3.8%	5.1%	6.4%
25	2.7	4.0	5.3	6.7
28	2.8	4.2	5.6	6.9
31	2.9	4.3	5.8	7.2
34	3.0	4.5	6.1	7.6
37	3.2	4.8	6.3	7.9
40	3.3	5.0	6.7	8.3
43	3.5	5.3	7.0	8.8
46	3.7	5.6	7.4	9.3
49	3.9	5.9	7.8	9.8

reposition your portfolio — that is, alter the level of diversification — to improve the overall return. Remember, when you fall below your break-even level, the cause may be either too little diversification or too much. The translation: You probably need to accept a higher level of risk in order to meet your minimum return requirements. The chart in Figure 1.3 summarizes break-even returns at various inflation and tax levels.

Pitfall #2: Failure to Monitor the Portfolio

The second common pitfall in diversification is the *failure to monitor* the portfolio. The need to review is constant, because no single decision concerning appropriate levels of diversification is going to remain applicable forever. Any change in the markets will affect the ongoing value of a particular product choice; any change in your income level will immediately change your short-term goals and objectives; and any change in available resources will require a re-evaluation of your diversification program. Such changes could include getting a raise or inheriting a large amount of cash; or on the negative side, losing your job or facing an unexpected large expense. These life events require that you take a second look at your entire portfolio. And since diversification is the foundation for your asset allocation plan, it is the inevitable starting point that has to occur as a response to change.

> **The essential policy you need to bring into portfolio management involves three phases:**
> **1. Definition**
> **2. Allocation**
> **3. Change**

These changes are themselves most important. It is the nature of investing to live with continual change. Wise investment policy requires that we deal with change perpetually. The inexperienced investor makes a mistake when he or she develops a plan for approaching the market, and then does not alter the plan when circumstances require it. The essential policy you need to bring into portfolio management involves three phases: (a) definition, (b) allocation, and (c) change.

In the definition phase, you identify goals and objectives, risk tolerance, and appropriate solutions that are a good match. In the allocation phase, you pick investment classification and products that address the different needs of specific goals. And in the change phase, you review your decisions continually. You change as circumstances change, moving between investment and product selections as required, and equally important, as your personal goals and objectives change. We are all evolving throughout our lifetimes, and it only makes sense that we enable our portfolio to evolve along with us. Otherwise, yesterday's plan quickly goes out of date.

Pitfall #3: Failure to Diversify

The next pitfall to avoid is *failure to diversify*. This does not mean only that you don't spread your capital around enough to avoid risk. It means, more significantly, that you attempt to diversify but do not achieve real risk reduction. The most common example is when all of your capital is invested in products with identical risk factors. Even buying shares of one mutual fund may not diversify your portfolio adequately. While the fund itself will invest in a broad spectrum of stocks or bonds, they will likely contain the same attributes. An aggressive growth fund will tend to select stocks that have good potential for growth, but those will be stocks that are more volatile than average. Thus, if the market suffers a broad decline, it is also likely that the fund's value will fall, perhaps to a greater degree than the overall market.

Another example of failure to diversify is placing too much capital into a single industry or in stocks sharing the same characteristics (meaning, of course, the same types of risks). The dot.com craze, for example, involved the same industry and the same or similar risk attribute: newly formed companies, many of which had never shown a net profit. Clearly, investing all of one's capital within that singular range of stocks was a failure to diversify, even when a dozen or more stocks were owned. History has demonstrated that a failure in the market can be both sudden and broad-based. Thousands of individual investors found that out the hard way in their decision to invest in dot.com companies. The same cyclical forces affect other sectors to one degree or another. Economic forces certainly influence price trends in technology, retail, utility, financial, and many other sectors.

Besides ensuring that your program of diversification does truly help you to avoid similar risks, it is equally important to avoid self-deception. Investors are optimists. It is easy to forget the importance of risk reduction when, for example, you are enamored today with one particular sector. You may convince yourself that all computer stocks are going to remain strong into the indefinite future, and that buying stock in several computer companies is adequate diversification—and that you will profit in all of your stocks. And then a single event like backlogs in the chip industry, a new product, a big lawsuit, or any other number of possible events, affect the whole sector and your portfolio declines—not just one stock, but *all* of your computer stocks. This all too common scenario is easily avoided by performing a realistic, but critical analysis of the nature of diversification and risk.

Pitfall #4: Timing Issues and Problems

Finally, *timing issues* contribute to the problems of designing a properly diversified portfolio. The actual diversification decision depends to some degree on current market conditions, and those conditions are going to change sooner or later. For example, you might develop a program based on allocation of your portfolio based on specific goals and objectives, and within that allocation design, you diversify based on current market conditions. You have selected particular stocks, for example, that you consider relatively safe long-term growth prospects. However, a few months later, market conditions or developing news changes your opinion about specific companies, and you need to make changes. For example, before 1999, most investors considered the Blue Chip companies universally safe investments. Companies like Xerox and General Electric were as unapproachable as Arthur Andersen in the accounting industry. However, the corporate scandals of 2000 through 2002 affected both of those companies, and the negative publicity has affected the stock in both. For example, General Electric stock lost nearly half its value between 2002 and the early part of 2003. The problems experienced by both of these companies may have had little to do with their long-term growth prospects, or even with the intrinsic value of their stock. However, the timing of the news made those stocks especially poor short-term investments.

Thus, if you had diversified your portfolio so that the Blue Chip portion (the safest in your mind) was invested for the moment in shares of Xerox and GE, a reconsideration would be required, if only because of the poor timing for holding those issues.

The next section expands on this discussion and examines asset allocation risks as they relate to and affect your portfolio and investment decisions.

Chapter 2

ASSET ALLOCATION RISKS

R isk is unavoidable. Every investor eventually comes to realize and accept this, and awareness of the nature of risks makes you a better, more effective, and more informed investor. In this chapter, the risks associated with asset allocation are explored and explained.

In the previous chapter, the specific attributes of diversification were demonstrated as the foundation of your asset allocation process. Remember the distinction between diversification and asset allocation. Once you have identified the specific goals and objectives of your financial plan, you allocate specific portions of your capital. The allocation segments may contain different risk elements, because the goals and objectives are themselves dissimilar. Within each allocated segment, you will want to diversify your portfolio to reduce market-specific and product-specific risks.

In this section, we will review allocation from several aspects: excessive diversification, market changes, anticipating change, using asset allocation to protect your position, investment volatility risk, fundamental volatility, and asset allocation in the post-Enron age.

When Diversification Is Excessive

In the last chapter, we reviewed the many pitfalls of diversification. Among these was the danger that you may over-diversify. Exactly how does this affect your overall allocation plan? Typically, the over-diversified portfolio is designed in an attempt to remove as much risk as possible. However, that also creates a situation in which opportunity for profit (the other side of the risk equation) can be taken by only a portion of the larger portfolio. The remainder, by design, will under-perform and the net effect is a lackluster performance record.

For example, let's assume that you have gone through the break-even analysis recommended in the last chapter, and you have decided that you need to earn 4.2% in your investment portfolio just to keep up with inflation and taxes. However, your portfolio has been diversified between nine different stocks. You have intentionally mixed high-volatility and low-volatility stocks with the purpose of diversifying. A review of the past year's performance shows the following returns (for the sake of illustration, we also assume that you invested the same amount of capital in each of these stocks):

Stock	Annual return
1	14.75%
2	10.25
3	8.50
4	4.65
5	2.15
6	- 4.75
7	- 6.65
8	- 8.25
9	-10.05

To find the net return average, add up the amounts in the annual return column and then divide the total by the number of stocks: 10.6 divided by 9 = 1.18%.

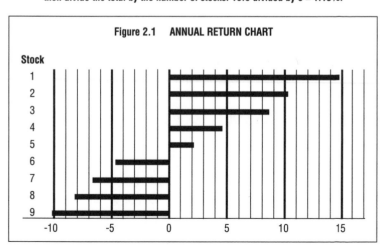

Figure 2.1   ANNUAL RETURN CHART

The net return in this example is 1.18%, well below the minimum requirement of 4.2%. In this case, the over-diversified portfolio did not work out. Only four of the nine issues exceeded the required return.

In this situation, you would need to review many of your assumptions. Did you pick stocks with similar risk attributes? Was it a mistake to diversify only within the stock market, or should some portion have been placed into a non-stock investment? Would performance have been more suitable in a mutual fund account?

While the illustration (see Figure 2.1) makes the point about diversification problems, it also relates to the larger question of asset allocation. As a starting point, you need to examine the goals and objectives underlying the portfolio decisions. Were your decisions appropriate, given the type of goal? Perhaps the very question of *how* you have allocated your resources should be accompanied with another: that is, *why* you selected (a) stocks as the appropriate venue, (b) the issues themselves and relative risk factors, and (c) the degree of capital placed into those issues.

> **The point to remember about excessive diversification is this: To the degree that it has a negative impact on overall returns, you need to strike a more effective balance between risk and return.**

The point to remember about excessive diversification is this: To the degree that it has a negative impact on overall returns, you need to strike a more effective balance between risk and return. That usually means narrowing diversification in terms of specific markets as well as issues. The stock market, of course, is a favorite choice for investors. However, consider mixing stocks and bonds (either via direct purchase or through using a balanced mutual fund); placing some portion of capital in a mortgage pool (debt rather than equity); mixing direct purchase of stocks with some regular mutual fund purchases; and selecting stocks of companies that participate in a dividend reinvestment plan (enabling you to achieve compound returns on dividend income). All of these steps are likely to strengthen your asset allocation program while doing away with the problems of excessive diversification.

Market Changes

Any market is going to be in a constant state of change. No investor should be surprised at sudden change, especially in the stock market. Real estate—especially directly owned—is far more stable on a day-to-day basis, but even supply and demand for housing is subject to ever-changing market forces.

> In developing your asset allocation plan, you need to understand the nature of change in the specific market, and to be ready to "ride out" the short-term changes.

Investors often bemoan the uncertainties of change. Of course, when markets fall, no one is happy, but even when markets rise, many missed opportunities become obvious, so investors, even though optimists in the general sense, also dislike change. However, it is the very nature of an investment opportunity to be accompanied with volatility. Risk and potential cannot be separated; they are typical characteristics of all worthwhile markets.

In developing your asset allocation plan, you need to understand the nature of change in the specific market, and to be ready to "ride out" the short-term changes. Using the stock market as an example, we all know that the most interesting stocks also tend to be very volatile. This can translate to big profits or equally big losses. Thus, the importance of allocating resources among dissimilar markets cannot be emphasized too much. The choices you make concerning where to invest should be based on your goals and objectives, selection of market choices with a full awareness of changes likely to occur, and of course, your own risk tolerance.

Your goals and objectives dictate the amount of change you are willing to tolerate. If you think about change as a form of uncertainty, then you can quantify a specific market or type of product more accurately. If your child is an infant and you wish to begin saving for college in 18 years, you can afford short-term volatility as long as you are certain about longer-term growth opportunities. If you are more conservative, you could invest in an area more stable than the stock market, but yielding less. In this case, you exchange uncertainty for lower overall yield.

Too many investors overlook the uncertainty of a market, assuming that a profit will be earned no matter what. Again, depending on your goals and objectives and the timing issues involved, you might be willing to live with the short-term uncertainties, or you might prefer to accept lower yields in exchange for more certainty (less risk).

Your risk tolerance level should be adjusted as part of your asset allocation plan, and probably will need to be adjusted many times throughout your lifetime. Risk tolerance is going to change as a matter of course whenever your own career and income status changes, and as you gain more experience in the markets. But even if you believe you have identified your current risk tolerance, a realistic review might be in order. If you incorporate the break-even analysis involving inflation and taxes, you might discover that you need to accept more risk than you previously thought, in order to match or beat the inflation and taxes problem.

Anticipating Change

As a starting point in determining how and why to allocate your financial resources, a wise policy is to expect and anticipate *change* as an inescapable attribute of investing. It is at the core of progress in all forms. Change is the means of profit and loss. If you were able to buy shares of stock in complete assurance that nothing would ever change in terms of safety, then that would also mean the market value of that stock would never change either.

The problem, of course, is that change sometimes means profit, and sometimes it means loss. And you have no way of knowing which will occur, other than by undertaking an intelligent and thorough approach to investment selection. In the stock market, that means combining fundamental analysis and timing, and accepting the fact that you will not win all of the time. Most investors consider themselves successful if they are right two out of three times; this is the nature of investing in the stock market more than anywhere else, where the potential for profit and loss is short-term and visible. It is so easy to trade shares on the public market that it is quite possible to double your money in one day, or to lose half of everything in half an hour. While most change in the market will be more gradual and not quite as extreme, the very possibility of such change—in either direction—is the source of so much interest in the stock market.

Acceptance of change also requires diligent management over your portfolio. You may allocate some assets to a low-yielding, insured savings account, and that requires virtually no maintenance at all. Another portion might be invested in a long-term bond, while requires very little maintenance; you need only to monitor periodically the bond rating to make sure the issuer continues to hold its investment grade status. Another portion could be invested in a GNMA (Government National Mortgage Association, also known as Ginnie Mae) mortgage pool, requiring some monitoring, but not daily. Finally, you may allocate assets to the stock market, either through mutual funds or direct purchase. That requires constant maintenance due to the potential for day-to-day changes, not just in price but in the strength and safety of the company itself.

While each and every allocation decision should be based primarily on your personal goals and objectives, it is important to recognize the varying degrees of monitoring needed, based on the volatility of a specific market. Most people—except the very risk adverse—will recognize the better than average potential in owning stocks, and along with that is the need to anticipate, monitor, and manage change.

Using Asset Allocation to Protect Your Position

The purpose of asset allocation must go beyond spreading resources among various and different forms of investment. That is only an advanced form of diversification. Instead, asset allocation should be thought of as a way to implement your goals and objectives.

This is a key point in the whole financial planning process. In order to understand how and why to plan, it isn't enough to simply allocate assets as it is so often done. We hear experts proclaiming that it is time to allocate more of your portfolio to stocks, for example. However, this is a senseless approach. Because you are different from anyone else in terms of your goals and objectives, risk tolerance, and experience, no one blanket decision can possibly apply. To allocate according to such generalizations is invariably a mistake.

You protect your investment position when allocation takes place as part of defining your goals and objectives. Allocation is the realization of the goal itself; by understanding the requirements of the goal, the solutions become more readily available, and the decisions you make in allocating your resources have a sensible base. So instead of considering asset allocation as a starting point for diversifying your portfolio, it makes perfect sense to define your goals and objectives, identify appropriate risk tolerance levels, and only then allocate resources to achieve your goals.

> **Instead of considering asset allocation as a starting point for diversifying your portfolio, it makes perfect sense to define your goals and objectives, identify appropriate risk tolerance levels, and only then allocate resources to achieve your goals.**

So many investors have the process backwards, even though the steps are apparent upon analysis. This is why so many portfolios fail and why so many investors have to struggle. There is an old bit of wisdom in the financial planning world that goes, "If you don't know where you're going, any road will get you there." In other words, the plan itself is the source for guidance, and that has to be based on definition, analysis, and decisions, not on any simple formula.

Investment Volatility Risk

Most investors equate market risk with price volatility, and for good reason. If you, like most investors, understand the stock market, you already know that price movement is the primary means for distinguishing one stock from another.

However, if you wish to allocate your stock portfolio on the basis of market risk (volatility), you should be aware that volatility often is misunderstood. Many investors use a standard volatility formula based on a stock's 52-week range. That formula calls for dividing the difference between high and low price, by the annual low. For example, assume that a stock's 52-week trading range has been 38 and 52 per share. The volatility formula is:

$$\frac{52 - 38}{38} = 36.8\%$$

In another example, a stock's trading range was between 26 and 21. Volatility is:

$$\frac{26 - 21}{21} = 23.8\%$$

This simple method for establishing volatility is not accurate; thus, using the information published in the financial press to determine the volatility of stocks is a poor way to identify the true volatility factor. The formula is inaccurate for several reasons:

1. It fails to distinguish between rising and declining trading range trends.

For example, one stock might be trending upward, while another with the same volatility factor has been declining throughout the year. The astute investor would interpret these price trends in much different ways. The differences are shown in Figures 2.2 (rising trend) and 2.3 (declining trend). There appear to be two distinct trends in these patterns, with both rising in Figure 2.2 and both declining in Figure 2.3. These make the point, however, that even when the volatility range is identical, it can be interpreted in very different ways depending upon the overall trend.

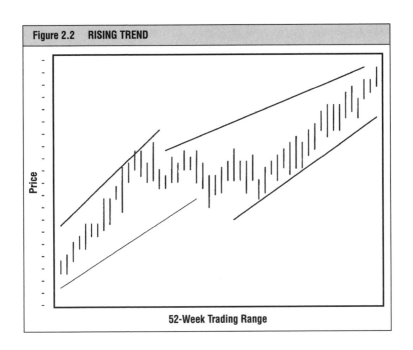

Figure 2.2 RISING TREND

Price

52-Week Trading Range

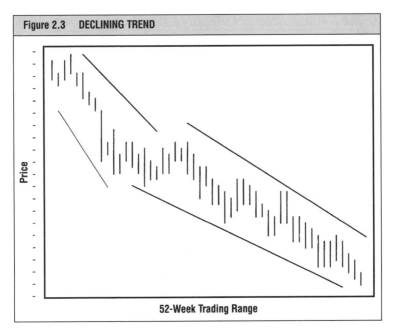

Figure 2.3 DECLINING TREND

Price

52-Week Trading Range

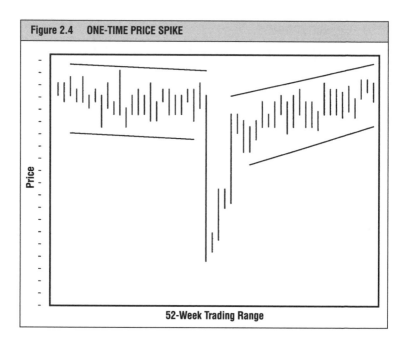

Figure 2.4 ONE-TIME PRICE SPIKE

Price

52-Week Trading Range

2. The formula does not identify upward or downward price spikes which are not typical of the trading range.

In this case, using the standard volatility formula could be quite inaccurate. An example of a price trend with a one-time price spike is shown in Figure 2.4. This could occur for any number of reasons not directly related to the company, such as a general market movement, a rumor about the company that later proved false, or a decision by a large mutual fund to sell its share of the stock. In the example, the full-year trading range was fairly narrow with the exception of the downward spike at mid-year. In this case, you would want to exclude the spike because it was not part of the established trading range and it appeared to have not affected or changed the range afterwards.

3. The 52-week formula includes recent pricing trends as well as outdated price trends (a full year ago).

This makes the comparison unreliable. To accurately judge volatility, it would make sense to (a) begin with the 52-week range using an online free charting service, (b) study the pricing pattern to determine whether the full 52-week period accurately reflects current trends in the stock, and (c) if a shorter period is justified, use more recent trends to judge volatility.

4. The picture may be distorted by earnings reports and other news during the full year.

As a general rule, it is an error to use a full 52 weeks for any sort of pricing trends, because older information is usually less reliable and does not reflect the *likely* future trend, nor the current volatility status. Given the possibility that interim events have made older price ranges irrelevant, it makes sense to use a shorter period to judge current volatility.

The past price trend is not going to indicate future prices with any reliability; this is an important aspect of any technical study. However, there is a tendency to believe that past trends do show how future price movement will occur. Because many Wall Street analysts come from the business world, they tend to believe that price predictions are as much a science as are business predictions. However, in business, you may rely on sales trends as well as known costs and expense levels to scientifically estimate future operations levels. In the stock market, prices move at the whim of many factors, some of which are wholly irrational. The art of trying to anticipate stock price movement apart from business trends in the company is elusive.

> As a general rule, it is an error to use a full 52 weeks for any sort of pricing trends, because older information is usually less reliable and does not reflect the likely future trend, nor the current volatility status.

The value of studying price volatility should not be ignored, but it is limited. Assuming that you look beyond the traditional formula and study recent price patterns, volatility is a valid method for selecting one risk level over another. For example, regardless of

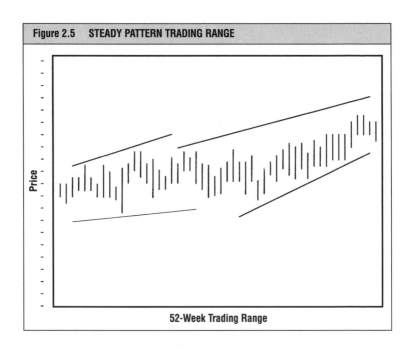

Figure 2.5   STEADY PATTERN TRADING RANGE

Price

52-Week Trading Range

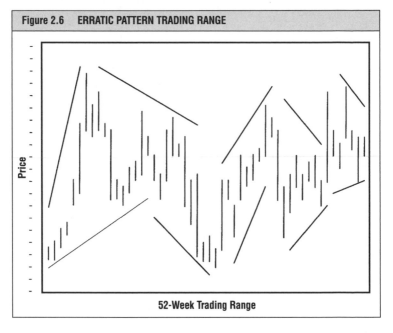

Figure 2.6   ERRATIC PATTERN TRADING RANGE

Price

52-Week Trading Range

the volatility percentage, consider the difference between two different stocks, one with a steady pattern and identifiable trading range, and the other showing an erratic trend. These differences are shown in Figures 2.5 and 2.6. In Figure 2.5, the trading range is consistent throughout the year with a gradual up-trend evident. In Figure 2.6, a more chaotic picture emerges, making it very difficult to predict future trend direction at all. These last two examples demonstrate the usefulness of volatility analysis for price; obviously, the erratic stock would be considered high-risk whereas the steady pattern would be lower-risk.

Clearly, price volatility is valuable. But to truly understand it and to properly allocate your assets on the basis of relative price risk, you need to analyze the true meaning of the past year's price movement, rather than applying an overall formula that does not take these variables into account.

> **Figures 2.5 and 2.6 demonstrate the usefulness of volatility analysis for price — the erratic stock would be considered high-risk whereas the steady pattern would be lower-risk.**

Fundamental Volatility

Another form of volatility, one that is usually ignored or forgotten, is "fundamental" volatility. While market volatility relates to the changes in stock prices, fundamental volatility refers to a company's reported sales and profits.

Investors like certainty in their investment earnings reports. Ironically, even those who accept considerable volatility in stock prices are often far more sensitive when earnings reports vary even slightly from forecasts. This desire for reliability is one of the factors that led to the well-publicized corporate scandals of 2001 and 2002. Responding in part to the desire for predictable earnings reports, many Wall Street analysts often gave out earnings reports based only on what they had been told by corporate officers. Those officers, whose compensation included incentive pay for keeping

> **Market volatility relates to the changes in stock prices, while fundamental volatility refers to a company's reported sales and profits.**

stock prices on the rise, then were motivated to cook the books. This can be accomplished through off-balance sheet transactions, deferring or capitalizing expenses, booking revenue too early, and a number of other creative but questionable practices.

The outcome of all of this was a dependable earnings report system. Many large companies reported healthy but gradual increases in sales, consistent dividend payments, and robust earnings. Of course, in the real world most business people know that financial outcomes are far more chaotic. Now that the rules have been tightened up for corporate officers, audit committees, and accounting firms, it is far more likely that a higher degree of fundamental volatility will occur in public earnings reports. Wall Street analysts have been largely discredited by their conflicts of interest and questionable earnings report methodology, so for those interested in allocating assets by levels of fundamental volatility, there may be a lot of opportunity.

Some companies will be characteristically low in fundamental volatility by the nature of their operating cycles, and others will tend to report widely diverse earnings from one quarter to another. For example, the retail industry has a 12-month cycle with the majority of its sales and profits occurring during the holiday season. Technology has a longer cycle, but it can be tracked in terms of the fundamentals, and the financial reports will reflect changes in that sector's cycles.

Asset Allocation in the Post-Enron Age

The tendency for different sectors to report varying degrees of fundamental volatility is an opportunity to exercise an important form of asset allocation. Without any doubt, this is an important form of risk to track, and you would not want to have your entire portfolio invested in a series of stocks whose fundamental volatility tended to follow the same patterns.

As a response to the corporate problems broadly known as "Enronitis" many important changes have taken place throughout the industry and regulation. The Sarbanes-Oxley Act has tightened up reporting and disclosure requirements, strengthening the whole regulatory environment. The major stock exchanges have enacted new rules for their member companies concerning the make-up of boards of directors and audit committees, ensuring an improved disclosure and reporting system. All of these changes make it more difficult for corporate officers to abuse their positions for self-enrichment. Changes in methods for providing and reporting stock options enhance these improvements. Analysts have to disclose conflicts of interest when their firms also operate as investment bankers for companies they recommend, and a separation between research and investment banking will eventually be implemented throughout the industry.

For investors, these changes are all significant. In the post-Enron age, you may expect to see a greater degree of fundamental volatility as companies and accounting firms shy away from "creative accounting" methods for reporting sales and profits. Investors are going to be more cautious for many years to come regarding putting too much capital at risk in the stock market, or even within diversified market programs. We should expect to see more self-imposed forms of asset allocation as investors become more conservative, at least for a few years.

There is a tendency for people to forget. A review of American

> **In the post-Enron age, you may expect to see a greater degree of fundamental volatility as companies and accounting firms shy away from "creative accounting" methods for reporting sales and profits.**

stock market history reveals that there is a cycle of scandal, price decline, and recovery. Depending upon the severity of the scandal, it may take several years for the markets to recover; however, the American economy remains strong even during recessions and political unrest. There is no doubt that we will again see a bull market and widespread optimism. It will be important for the wise investor to remember that, even when markets are on the rise, asset allocation should always be employed as a wise strategy for portfolio management.

Chapter 3

THE PERSONALIZED PROGRAM

Once you fully understanding the elements of risk involved with all forms of investing, the next step is to begin putting a personal financial plan into effect. That requires definition of goals and objectives, identification of acceptable risk tolerances, and an analysis of all needs as restricted by available resources, time horizon, and family status.

Some portfolio theories apply formulas to determine how to allocate assets. However, it is more likely that you will want to tailor your program specifically to your current needs and that you will modify your assumptions many times during your lifetime. Some of the popular methods for determining how to allocate assets are summarized below. If any of these are used, they should serve only as a starting point and not as an easy solution to the ways that you will need to exercise asset allocation.

The *cash flow needs model* matches your income against expenses to identify the amount you have available to invest each month. From there, the decisions about how much to allocate into specific risk and market areas is to be determined by age, level of available cash, and risk tolerance—as well as by the specific goals and objectives.

Another approach is *tactical asset allocation.* While the first method is driven by income and available resources, this method is more appropriate when you have an established pool of funds. Under the tactical theory, you or your advisor will switch between stocks, bonds, cash and other allocated markets depending on ever-emerging circumstances. This method assumes that it is possible to call markets effectively, and that assumption is questionable. For those interested in developing an allocation program driven by goals and objectives rather than by market conditions, this approach would seem too speculative.

The *brokerage house model* depends on recommendations from a broker for allocating a portfolio among stocks, bonds, cash, and often derivatives as well. Only those with great confidence in a brokerage house would be advised to employ this model. Its primary flaw is that it is driven by the brokerage house's perception of market conditions more than by the individual goals and objectives of each investor.

The *common stocks for the long run* method is not allocation at all. This method assumes that all of your money should be allocated to common stocks in the belief that, in the long run, the stock market will outperform other markets. You could diversify within this method, of course, but when you allocate funds 100%, you are not allocating at all. This method usually enjoys a short-term popularity when stocks are climbing rapidly in a broad-based bull market, but it is virtually unheard of when stocks are falling.

The *"100 less your age" model* is based on two beliefs. First, you will live to be 100 and second, you will become less risk tolerant as you age. The portfolio is divided strictly between equity investments and fixed income. When you are 40, for example, you would invest 60% of your portfolio in equity, and 40% in fixed

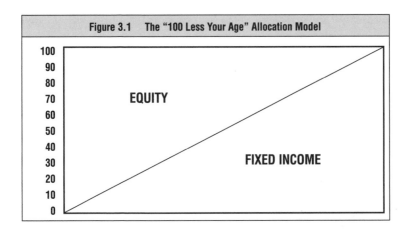

Figure 3.1   The "100 Less Your Age" Allocation Model

EQUITY

FIXED INCOME

income. By age 50, you would split half and half between the two areas. And at age 95, you would have 5% in equity and 95% in fixed income. The problems with this method are obvious: the formula applies on a single assumption, ignoring stock market and interest rate conditions, not to mention your personal preferences in managing your portfolio.

Finally, the *financial objectives method* mandates that your asset allocation plan is based on your goals and objectives. This is the only sensible approach, because it will be tailored to you individually and can be altered as your personal and family status changes. Under this method, you can establish your needs for an emergency cash reserve based on current income and expenses and then define a number of goals and objectives. Under the financial objectives method, you are able to allocate your portfolio according to your time horizon, income level, and risk tolerance. As part of a comprehensive financial plan, you will also be able to budget for needed forms of insurance (life, health,

> **These methods should serve only as a starting point and not as an easy solution to the ways that you will need to exercise asset allocation.**

disability, homeowners, auto) and coordinate all aspects of your plan with the asset allocation strategy.

Identifying Specific Goals and Needs

The first step in any financial plan is defining *why* you need to invest. Where are you going, financially speaking? This beginning phase often is more difficult than you might think, for several reasons:

- Spouses often have not discussed their goals and objectives and might discover that they do not agree on priorities
- Some people have never thought ahead far into the future, assuming that events like retirement are so distant that no planning is needed today
- If an individual or young couple does not yet own a home or have children, the urgency of planning is not apparent

With these basic observations in mind, remember that planning is not only essential for everyone's future; it is also wise to begin as soon as possible. The longer the time available to plan throughout your working years, the more effectively you will be able to meet your goals and objectives.

To begin, a good exercise is to write down the three to five most important goals that you wish to reach financially. These may include saving for a child's college education, for a down payment on your first home or to accelerate mortgage payments on the home you already own, setting up your own business so that you can change careers and become independent, and of course, saving for your retirement. Everyone will have their own goals in addition to these more obvious ones. A husband and wife should write down their goals individually and then compare notes. They often will find that they have some conflicts to resolve. Many financial plans begin by coordinating dissimilar goals held by husband and wife. The plan will only work well if both sides are able to include their goals within the plan.

Use the worksheet shown in Table 3.1 to document your personal goals and objectives.

TABLE 3.1   PERSONAL INVESTMENT GOALS

Name_____ Date_____

Goals, in order of importance:

1._____
_____
_____
_____

                    Estimated time horizon_____

2._____
_____
_____
_____

                    Estimated time horizon_____

3._____
_____
_____
_____

                    Estimated time horizon_____

4._____
_____
_____
_____

                    Estimated time horizon_____

5._____
_____
_____
_____

                    Estimated time horizon_____

Note that each goal provides room for a complete description as well as a time horizon. Setting a deadline for yourself in terms of months or years is essential. This defines (a) the time you allow yourself to accumulate funds you will need to reach the goal, (b) a financial roadmap of your current perceptions about how you expect this goal to be achieved, and (3) a test of how realistic your goal is, given the limitations of your personal assets, income and savings.

If you are married, you and your spouse should each fill out this form. The comparison of goals and deadlines will be revealing and will save you both a lot of time and trouble. By bringing up conflicts and differences at the *beginning* of the planning process, you will better know how both sides can be allowed to reach their priority goals. This definition phase will also dictate how and when you will need to allocate your assets to position yourselves properly.

A *goal* is the "big picture" of what you hope to achieve through your investment plan. The *objective* is the method by which you ensure that your plan stays on track. Goals and objectives go together and cannot really be viewed separately. The comprehensive financial plan requires that you have both.

With the goals agreed upon, or at least acknowledged at this point, the next step is to break down the specific ideas about how to get from here to there. We may call these steps "objectives." The distinction between goals on the one hand and objectives on the other is not always clear; many people use the terms to mean the same thing. We make a distinction, however. A *goal* is the "big picture" of what you hope to achieve through your investment plan—retirement, college education, purchasing primary and vacation homes, starting your own business, getting out of debt, and so forth. The *objective* is the method by which you ensure that your plan stays on track. Objectives include purchasing the right kinds of insurance to offset the unexpected loss, prepaying your mortgage so it will be paid off by the deadline of an important goal, and identifying the proper allocation of your portfolio. In other words, objectives are properly part of the process related to your goals. Goals and objectives go together and cannot really be viewed separately. The comprehensive financial plan requires that you have both.

Your goals will be affected not only by your hopes and dreams, but also by many other important factors. These include your age, education, income, risk tolerance level, investment experience, and family status (married, single, number of children, etc.). As time goes on, your goals will need to be adjusted for major changes. These may include single people getting married, the birth of children, buying a home, losing a job or switching careers, divorce, death, and retirement, to name only a few. All of these are major changes and have to be expected to radically change your priorities. Thus, goals and objectives cannot be established and then left alone. As living beings, we are all in a constant state of change, and that will continue. Many people desire stability and certainty in their lives and are able to achieve some degree of that type of safety in some respects. But no one can control those events that impose themselves upon our lives. So, for proper planning, goals and objectives have to be reviewed regularly, and they have to include the following features related to setting objectives:

- ***Anticipation of change***: the recognition that the unexpected events are the ones that define whether or not we succeed in our financial plan

- ***Insurance against loss***: the required protective methods everyone needs for those catastrophic losses we might suffer, such as fire, auto accident, illness or accident, disability, or the loss of life of a family member

- ***Risk analysis***: an ongoing critical review of your portfolio with the knowledge that yesterday's assumptions might not apply today and tomorrow

- ***Asset allocation review***: the need to monitor your portfolio and, when required, shift from one investment sector to another, due to market conditions, changes in your goals, adjustments in risk tolerance, or a combination of all of these elements

The setting of goals and objectives, like all stages of your financial plan, cannot take place in isolation, nor is it unchanging. Your life goals may remain unchanged, but specific objectives will evolve over time. Most experts have acknowledged that financial planning is not just a function to be done once; it is a process that guides you throughout your life, involving the definition, monitoring, and changing of objectives and, based on major life events, often setting new goals and changing priorities.

Allocation of Available Resources

Your financial resources — income as well as savings and other investments — will ultimately determine how and when you will be able to put your plan into effect. These resources are restricting factors that affect the time horizon of your goals. For example, you might desire to purchase a home immediately and have it paid off in ten years. Realistically, however, you know it is going to take a few years to save up a down payment and achieve an income level adequate to gain financing, and then, more likely, 15 to 30 years to pay off a mortgage.

There are two priorities to remember about asset allocation. First is the desired allocation of resources based on identified goals, and second is the restriction of resources that inhibits your ability to put the plan into effect and achieve your goals as quickly as possible. Coordinating two requirements, which often conflict with one another, is going to characterize financial planning for everyone just starting out in their plan.

Once you have identified your goals and objectives, you next need to determine how to assign investment assets to each goal. The necessity of allocation becomes apparent at this point: because every goal has its own time horizon and other characteristics, it is also likely that you will need to allocate assets in a dissimilar manner. It serves no purpose to identify goals and then invest without matching investment types.

For example, you might decide that a long-term bond (or bond fund) will be appropriate to begin saving today for an infant child whose college education will begin 18 years from now. An even more conservative approach would be to purchase an endowment insurance policy. In comparison to these goals, you might further decide that your retirement assets should be invested in aggressive equity investments, via stocks directly owned or through mutual fund shares. A more sophisticated investor may also decide to devote a portion of the portfolio to more speculative investments like futures or options, but only if appropriate to the specific and identified goal.

So each allocation decision is specifically identified with and matched to a specific goal. The various levels of allocation will have their own risk attributes, some more conservative than others, all based on the nature of the goal. A younger person or family will have more time to retirement, so a longer time horizon will mean you can alter your risk tolerance accordingly. However, if you are in your 40s and beginning a retirement plan today, you cannot afford losses in your portfolio, so you are more likely to employ lower-risk alternatives and allocate your assets accordingly. For example, you might decide to accelerate mortgage payments so that your house will be paid off in 15 years instead of 30. This reduces interest expenses and will also reduce your monthly income needs when you do retire.

These many methods for allocating assets will vary not only by your risk tolerance and time horizon, but also by your personal preference and investing experience. Some investors have lost a lot of investment dollars in the stock market and do not want to repeat that experience. Does this mean they should avoid the stock market? No, but it does point to the need for more thoughtful diversification accompanied by thorough fundamental analysis — as a starting point for allocating assets to equities. The identification of

> **Asset allocation is a tool for managing your personal goals and objectives, not as a trite exercise in the *concept* of financial planning, but as an indispensable tool within your portfolio.**

both market price and fundamental volatility serve as starting points in identifying risk factors for specific stocks or stock market sectors. In picking stocks for your portfolio, also remember that short-term value change is going to occur but what most goals will mandate is going to be long-term growth. Thus, picking equities and expecting speculative short-term profits is high-risk. Most speculators lose, even if they do get occasional profits. Consistency is very difficult in that game; so even if you do return to the stock market after being out, be sure to study various equities and diversify your holdings based on analysis and comparison.

Asset allocation is a tool for managing your personal goals and objectives, not as a trite exercise in the *concept* of financial planning, but as an indispensable tool within your portfolio. Some investors believe that tracking price movements through charts is the key to success, while others try to time decisions and allocate heavily in equity, debt, real estate, and other markets based on tracking economic, political, and market news. Remember, though, that no matter what techniques you employ to try and beat the averages, short-term cyclical changes are always difficult to identify. Even though some people claim their system is foolproof (chartists are one example) the fact is that any system will provide value and guidance, but none are going to ensure short-term market success. So as part of your asset allocation program, maintain your long-term perspective, remembering time horizons and goal deadlines. Don't be too concerned with short-term change. Pick an intelligent strategy for allocating your assets between various markets based on your goals, and then track changes in your goals to adjust your allocation program.

Matching Resources with Goals

The need for allocating assets based on goals is always logical, in theory. In practice, however, resources are invariably limited. Anyone with a limited investment budget and portfolio needs to ensure that those limited resources match the priorities established when you set your goals.

A problem, however, arises when you attempt to set the priority itself. Which is the most important, a child's college education or buying your first home? Your current insurance requirements or retirement a few decades from now? In most families, available financial resources are rarely adequate to address *all* of the priorities expressed through goals. A solution is needed that sets priorities more keenly, without ignoring the importance of any goals.

Part of this problem requires rational evaluation. Are you being practical? It might not make sense to want an early retirement, your own business, a college education and a mortgage-free home all before the age of 40. While those goals make a nice wish list, the resources simply are not there. When you consider ongoing budgetary demands, including housing, food, insurance, utilities, taxes, and consumer debt, you may have to struggle just to free up a few dollars each month to make any investments.

For many families in this situation, the single plan involves a combination of tax-deferred retirement savings (combining employer-provided benefits and IRA accounts, for example) with a very modest starting-out program. For example, you might be able to afford only to place funds into a mutual fund each month, hoping that a consistent program will later evolve into a more sophisticated and diversified financial plan.

The reality of current income limitations will also limit your ability to allocate assets as effectively as you would like and to address the various goals and objectives you have expressed at the start of your plan. So a good starting point is to do what you can in a consistent, disciplined manner. This works well unless the unexpected comes along, and that can take several forms. The unplanned car repair or accident is relatively minor compared to an unplanned pregnancy, a serious illness, the death of a family member, a divorce, or the loss of your primary job. All of these events naturally throw your long-term plan into disarray as priorities are turned upside down.

> **Anyone with a limited investment budget and portfolio needs to ensure that those limited resources match the priorities established when you set your goals.**

In the event of the unpleasant life surprise, the longer-term question of achieving financial goals is put aside, at least until you recover. However, if you have embarked on planning your financial future to the extent possible, you will be better equipped to deal with the emergency, even if it means having to suspend everything else. A little planning is better than none and, assuming that everything goes according to the plan itself, it will lead to an expanded asset allocation program later.

You cannot plan for every possible emergency. However, many can be anticipated through the following essentials:
- Insurance
- Emergency reserve funds
- Using professional help

You cannot plan for every possible emergency. However, many can be anticipated through the following essentials:

Insurance is an absolute requirement for every adult. If you have dependents, you need to insure the life of the primary breadwinner. The guideline should always be to insure against any loss you cannot afford. If you are the sole income-earner in your family, you need life and disability plans to cover your family's budget each month (remembering other benefits such as survivor's social security, for example). You also need health insurance for all family members, auto and homeowners, and additional coverage for any assets you own not covered by the standard policies. As a beginning of your financial plan, be sure that you have budgeted for all of the insurance coverage you need to offset as many possible catastrophic losses as possible.

Emergency reserve funds should be set aside as a high priority in every family. This fund provides you with budget relief in the event you lose your job or face an unexpected expense not covered in your monthly budget. The emergency reserve can help you to stay on course with your financial plan, at least temporarily. Some advisors suggest putting aside six months' net income, less any unemployment benefits you would receive. For many families, barely able to put aside a modest investment each month in a savings account or mutual fund, a six-months' emergency reserve may not be practical. However, in that case, it is unlikely that a more advanced financial plan will be possible either, until income levels are improved.

Using professional help is always essential, especially if you have little or no experience in investing. Your advisor should be experienced in the areas where you need help, and may need to refer you to other experts as well. You and your spouse should have wills, so you will need to consult with an estate attorney; you will want a knowledgeable insurance agent; and of course, your financial planner should act as coordinator for documenting your entire plan in all of its aspects, including helping you to establish budgets for the various needs you face.

How Personal Situations Evolve Over Time

Every investor needs to operate within the limitations of their personal resources, experiences, and of course, goals. These three elements, working together, ultimately determine the shape of your financial plan.

All of these elements also have to be expected to evolve. None of them remain stagnant. It is a mistake to develop a comprehensive financial plan in the belief that it is going to serve as a guiding principle throughout your entire life, or even over the next ten years. It is far more likely that in the future, your point of view, circumstances, and life direction will have shifted significantly enough so that today's financial plan will be out of date. In the desire to achieve certainty and stability, some investors have put a lot of effort into identifying all of the essential elements they need, situations they will face, and goals they want to meet for the rest of their lives. This cannot be done. Your financial plan should serve as an outline of what you assume and believe today; the approach

> Your financial plan should serve as an outline of what you assume and believe today; the approach itself is a worthwhile discipline for the unending process of review, fine-tuning, and reaction to the unexpected. And remember, you don't know what changes are going to occur in future markets or in your life.

itself is a worthwhile discipline for the unending process of review, fine-tuning, and reaction to the unexpected. And remember, you don't know what changes are going to occur in future markets or in your life.

Personal Resources

Your savings, investments, and income are going to change in the future in unpredictable ways. As a starting point, most people budget their income so that they can invest a specific amount each month. They also assume future rates of inflation and target return on investment, all based on the primary assumption that the future is well understood. However, consider the range of possible events that could change all of those assumptions, for better or for worse. These include loss of a job, a promotion, the death of a spouse, unexpected medical bills, a lawsuit, or a large inheritance, just for a few examples. Each of these potential, and perhaps unexpected, outcomes would change *all* of today's assumptions concerning current and future resources.

Experiences

You grow in many ways, of course, and experience changes you. This is not only true in your personal life, but also in the way you approach investing. Every market experience affects your risk tolerance, and every success or failure adds a new dimension to the way you view a specific market. If you lost money investing in a dot.com company a few years ago, or if you put all of your portfolio in Enron stock at the beginning of the year 2000, or if your mutual funds lost 75% of their value, then you certainly have a vastly different outlook about the market today than you did before you lost so much of your equity. On the other hand, if you have made profits in well-selected equities, diversified your portfolio effectively, and made profits consistently, then those experiences only reinforce your system. Everyone changes on the basis of what they learn. It may be dangerous for first-time investors to enter the market, especially if they meet with initial success. Proceeding on the naïve assumption that profiting is an easy matter, they set themselves up for much larger and more painful losses later. Experienced investors know how to mitigate risks by moving money around in different types of equities. For example, you may allocate varying portions of your stock portfolio in blue chips, small-cap, foreign issues, and IPOs. That is one form of diversification within an equity portfolio. If you are more experienced, you might hedge long positions with put options, enhance income through covered calls, and use options in other ways. With experience, you learn the true nature of market risk, but you also learn new ways to diversify and make use of market possibilities.

Goals

You cannot expect today's goals to remain unchanged forever. It simply doesn't happen. When you look back 10 years, you know you have changed in many ways, and it is also likely that your goals have evolved as well. For example, a young career-minded person might dream of being a CEO or starting a company and going public. However, with business world experience, those dreams might evaporate. The same person might decide within a few years that a better course would be to work toward achieving a safe, secure, well-paying middle management position. A few years later, the idea of early retirement and becoming self-employed might be more appealing. In other words, experience and exposure invariably changes everyone, in unexpected ways. With youth comes passion, and ideas are firmly held and believed. Within a few years, though, and with a little more maturity, the same person abandons the youthful idea and takes another look around. The dream of being the first human to plant their feet on Mars is replaced with the desire to have their feet firmly planted right here on Earth. The desires and dreams of humans are the driving forces that propel us all; however, those dreams have to evolve or they become outdated and unrealistic. This is as true in your life dreams as it is in the investment world.

Investment Needs Versus Risk Tolerance

As part of your asset allocation program, you will constantly work to reconcile the conflicts between what you need to achieve in your portfolio — your investment needs — and your own risk tolerance level. If your portfolio does not perform according to the goals you establish (i.e., meeting or beating your after-tax and after-inflation break-even point) you need to assess whether your risk tolerance standards are realistic.

This problem is challenging because, in an allocated portfolio, not *all* risks are going to be identical. Based on specific goals and objectives and as an attribute of an asset allocation program, you will expose a portion of your assets to higher or lower risks than the average. No one is expected to achieve an identical and singular risk level within a diversified portfolio. By the very nature of allocation, it is desirable to live with a varied program of risks. Remember, risk is the opposite side of profit opportunity, so if you want to be exposed to a variety of profit scenarios, that also means you need to diversify risk.

> If your portfolio does not perform according to the goals you establish (i.e., meeting or beating your after-tax and after-inflation break-even point), you need to assess whether your risk tolerance standards are realistic.

So when you have defined your risk tolerance level, it is important to make distinctions based on your goals and objectives. You cannot allocate assets and define your whole portfolio with a generalization concerning risk; it is far more likely that as you effectively allocate assets, you will experience a broader—and desirable—range. So what do you do to fix the problem if and when a part of your allocated assets falls below expectations? Remember the following guidelines:

- *The under-performance could be temporary; remember to think long-term.* Any investment program has to be designed for long-term averages. It isn't realistic to expect to match or beat your goal each and every quarter or year. As long as you have allocated assets wisely, based on proper analysis and study, and as long as your initial assumptions remain valid, go for averages rather than concentrating on today's results. However, if your portfolio under-performs every year for three years or more, you could have a different problem; check the other items in the list below.

- **An adjustment, perhaps only a minor one, could fix the problem.** Some assumptions concerning risk tolerance and asset allocation need to be fine-tuned now and then. For example, you might pick a healthy stock sector but time your decisions poorly, meaning you went in at the wrong point in the cycle. A movement between companies within a single sector, or diversifying a portion into a more robust sector, could improve your averages.

- **You might need to move an allocated segment elsewhere.** The cycles of the market can be applied to individual stocks or sectors as well as to the market as a whole. It is most likely when you are invested in equities that the time comes to move an allocated segment from one series of equities to another, either in whole or in part. You cannot ignore the cycles, and a reliable program of fundamental analysis can be used to identify when the signal changes from "hold" to "sell" in your case.

- **You might need to review and change your risk tolerance assumptions.** Finally, you need to be able to critically analyze your own assumptions concerning risk. Remembering that you need to continually strive to make or beat your break-even point, yesterday's risk tolerance assumptions could be out of date today. This can cause your portfolio, or a portion of it, to under-perform. The problem may be due to a combination of changed markets, a weak economy, and the need to alter your risk tolerance due to changed personal circumstances and experience. For example, a stock portfolio's overall return can be vastly improved through a covered call options program, but only if you are experienced enough in the options market to know how to manage such a program. Less experienced investors are not suited for advanced strategies in investing, but as you advance in your market knowledge, it is ever more likely that you will be able to employ a broader range of strategies, hedge risks, and improve profits overall.

Risk Tolerance and How It Changes Over Time

Just as goals and objectives grow as you do, so will your risk tolerance levels. When you first begin investing, basic products are appealing, and understandably so. Because beginning investors usually have very little capital to invest, they are especially risk adverse. So as a starting point, they are attracted to insured savings accounts, conservative growth mutual funds or money market funds, and treasury securities. However, as investors gain experience in different markets *and* as their income and savings grow, there is an accompanying tendency for risk tolerance to expand as well.

The more experienced investor may actually become more conservative as an increased pot of investment capital becomes available. This is more true today than in the past, due to the unexpected and very costly shake-out in the dot.com industry, in which many inexperienced investors failed to recognize the importance of diversification. This lesson was reinforced in 2001 and 2002 with story after story of corporate scandals. Enron and many other companies, whose officers had been abusing their power since the mid-90s, were able to escape punishment because of a lax regulatory environment. In the mid- to late-90s the economy was strong and the stock market went up without coming down. In that time, the SEC and other regulators had little political support for increased budgets in their oversight and enforcement departments. Thus, once the problems were revealed, many years of abuse came to the surface within a few months.

Certainly, anyone who had trusted the audited financial statements of those companies whose reports turned out to be false and anyone who took the advice of Wall Street analysts was likely to lose money. As a consequence, some investors who started out as fairly aggressive learned a hard lesson and became overly conservative.

There should be some balance in the approach to risk tolerance, however. It does not make sense to apply an all-or-nothing approach to investing; in fact, that is a destructive approach. If you are too conservative, your capital loses spending power. As long as your net return does not match or beat your tax/inflation break-even level, your portfolio will not maintain its value. Of equal importance, an overly aggressive and speculative approach to investing invariably leads to unacceptable losses. The undiversified portfolio, or one in which reckless speculation is taking place, might profit in the short term. However, the vast majority of aggressive investors end up losing consistently.

The solution, of course, is to review constantly, even after carefully defining today's acceptable risk tolerance level. Be willing to adjust risk tolerance as you gain experience and as your income and resources change as well. Also remember that risk tolerance should be specifically designed to match the allocated assets within your portfolio. As part of the definition phase of objectives, identify what you consider an appropriate level of risk.

Some asset allocation methods depend on the formula approach, mandating that you split up your portfolio based on your age or some random method. The problem, of course, is that the formula approach does not address *your* situation, nor does it allow for change over time. You may decide that a long-term program for a young child's college education fund should be invested very conservatively, but that your own retirement account should be far more aggressive. So *risk* is not just an attribute of a diversified portfolio. It should serve as one of the defining factors that indicates how to allocate your assets

> **Review constantly, even after carefully defining today's acceptable risk tolerance level. Be willing to adjust risk tolerance as you gain experience and as your income and resources change as well. Also remember that risk tolerance should be specifically designed to match the allocated assets within your portfolio.**

and which investments are suitable, given all of the aspects of the decision: your own experience, age, income and assets, and of course, the risk/reward level.

The concept of "risk tolerance" usually considers only one-half of the equation. The higher the risk, the higher the potential profit. So when investors say, "I want as little risk as possible," that does not always mean that they are willing to accept the corresponding lower than average return on their investment. In fact, as unrealistic as it may be, some people believe they can have a combination of very low risk and very high profits. Obviously, this is flawed thinking. This is where more thorough definition is valuable.

Those who believe they have a low risk tolerance may, in fact, identify that with part of their portfolio. At the same time, it is also possible that a different allocation of assets would be appropriately identified as suitable for a higher level of risk tolerance. The more you examine this question, and the more fully you address the issue of risk *and* reward (and not only risk), the better your chances for success in managing your portfolio.

Tailoring Your Individual Strategy

The key to effective asset allocation is to consider it as a highly personalized process, rather than as a formula that can be applied once. It has to be personalized because your goals are yours alone, your time horizon depends on your age and income, and your risk tolerance has to rule your portfolio decisions.

The attempt to arrive at a formula does not address individual needs. Just as someone might recommend investing in a particular product without knowing anything about you, applying a formula for asset allocation based on market conditions or other criteria is not appropriate. To do so assumes that every investor is the same, that the allocation is proper in all situations, and that all risk tolerance levels and goals are the same.

Asset allocation is not a simple process either. Some investors desire simplicity and low risk, but they also desire the certainty of profits. These two opposing desires conflict with one another, of course. So on the risk side, investors seek simplified methods of diversifying their portfolios, while also trying to take advantage of short-term profit opportunities. Ironically, this approach exposes investors to high risk while lowering the chances for consistent profits. The inexperienced investor will view asset allocation as a high-level form of diversification. However, while the well-managed portfolio is diversified properly, asset allocation is really the process by which you select risks that work given a specific goal. This point is often overlooked by those investors attracted to the formula approach.

Your portfolio design will reflect your risk tolerance, and the methods you use to allocate assets should always be ruled by the goal itself—within the well-defined elements of risk, time horizon, your own investment experience and market conditions. Using the stock market as an example, you can tailor your portfolio in the following ways:

> **The key to effective asset allocation is to consider it as a highly personalized process, rather than as a formula that can be applied once.**

- moving allocated assets between sectors based on anticipation of cyclical changes

- diversifying within a particular sector or among stocks in different sectors

- using put options to insure long positions when you want to hold shares of stock, but you are concerned that prices have run up too quickly, and shares currently are over-priced

- using covered call options to enhance portfolio profits, assuming your investing experience makes this choice a suitable one for you

- moving funds out of the market temporarily (i.e., to a money market fund) when you think the market is over-bought and you expect a broad-based price decline

- diversifying by purchase of index options to take advantage of broad-based price movement in either direction

The essential point to remember about asset allocation is that it is a highly personalized program. It only works if you take that approach. Within any form of investing, there may be a number of ways to allocate assets and to diversify to protect yourself against a range of risks.

Chapter 4

MISCONCEPTIONS ABOUT
ASSET ALLOCATION

Every investor views the portfolio from a unique perspective. Your own point of view is the sum of your experiences, your attitudes toward wealth building, your individual goals, age, income, family status, maturity, and even your non-financial priorities.

If developing a financial plan is a very high priority for you, then developing the means for protecting your resources and reaching your goals will be something you take very seriously. That means you have to be willing to put in the time to research investments, monitor markets and products, and keep yourself up to date. There really are no easy ways to accumulate wealth unless you inherit it. If you, like most investors, have to depend on your own skill as an investor, then asset allocation is a valuable process, and it can help you to define your priorities.

Looking for the Magic Bullet

One approach to investing is to constantly search for a secret, some easy way to wealth. The get-rich-quick concept is broadly appealing, as witnessed by the number of sales pitches aimed at that idea. For a small investment, you can learn the secrets of getting fast riches.

That is as unlikely as the diet plans promising that you can lose weight without exercise and while eating anything you like.

Realistically, we all know that is not possible; however, those ads persist as well. For the investor, accumulating wealth is a process of hard work, facing and accepting risk, and even experiencing losses. The key, however, is to develop a system that allows you to earn a profit more often than you suffer a loss—and not to guarantee fast riches, easy profits, and no risk.

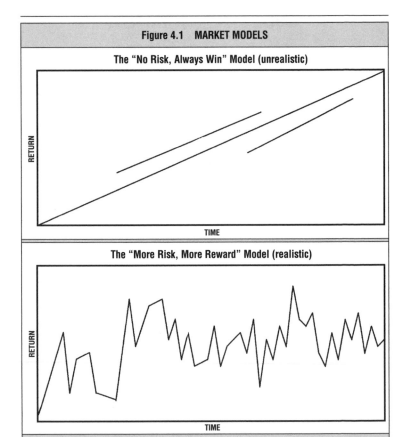

Figure 4.1 MARKET MODELS

The "No Risk, Always Win" Model (unrealistic)

RETURN

TIME

The "More Risk, More Reward" Model (realistic)

RETURN

TIME

An unrealistic expectation is to assume no real market risk. The belief that value will always rise no matter what, is a dangerous one, but a fairly common one as well. In practice, however, we know that risk and return are erratic and, while the overall return on your portfolio might be consistent over time, the short term is quite chaotic. The greater the price volatility in the stock, the higher the market risk.

One of the persistent myths on Wall Street is that there are ways to beat the system. Whether you track chart patterns, look for hidden signals in financial statements, or invest based on which side wins the Super Bowl, the "secret system" has the same appeal as the fountain of youth of past centuries. It is myth, but many people go off in search of it.

Asset allocation is an intelligent approach to long-term wealth building. To those who fancy the possibilities of fast wealth, asset allocation is a boring idea, one that promises nothing but long-term profits and constant monitoring. However, those who use boring but effective methods to manage their portfolios discover the only real secret to wealth building: success is the result of hard work.

> A financial plan is a process developed to serve your individual needs. The professional planner understands that you and your family are not like any other, and that your goals and objectives have to serve as the starting point for building your plan.

Personal Financial Planning

The process of asset allocation is a part of the comprehensive financial planning process. Planning itself is a highly individual process. Anyone who approaches you with a formula financial plan, who does not first evaluate your personal goals, time horizon, family status, risk tolerance, income, and experience, is not offering you any real financial planning.

A financial plan is a process developed to serve *your* individual needs. The professional planner understands that you and your family are not like any other, and that your goals and objectives have to serve as the starting point for building your plan. Asset allocation is the process by which you execute your action plan. No other method will work. It is not a simple process, nor does it remain the same. A professional financial planner works with you to establish the means of identifying how and what you need, the "getting from here to there" of the financial planning process. Asset allocation is the vehicle for developing a portfolio based on your goals and objectives, a process that—like all aspects of financial planning—has to be tailored to your own needs, *and* that will have to be modified over time.

Allocation as a Key to Effective Planning

Why is asset allocation so essential to portfolio management? Isn't that really a more involved process used by mutual fund managers?

The origins of asset management were indeed formulated at the institutional level. The mutual fund and insurance industries both manage a large and diversified portfolio. The insurance industry applies actuarial principles to risk management, and mutual fund managers study the markets and individual companies to select appropriate risks. However, the concept of asset allocation does not have to serve as a complex method for spreading risks among many different markets. In fact, on an individual level it should be far more simple.

You may decide that your primary goal is saving for retirement, and that you will most likely achieve that by investing all of your cash in technology stocks. You could be right over the long term, assuming that (a) technology stocks will serve as a consistent growth sector, (b) that you pick the right stocks to beat the averages, (c) that you time your purchases well, and (d) that technology itself does not change in the future to make current company products obsolete.

This is a big list of assumptions. Many things can go wrong, including product obsolescence. Not many years ago, for example, Polaroid was a highly respected company whose products were recognized as state-of-the-art. The instant photo technology was a popular idea at one time. However, Polaroid did not maintain its competitive edge when digital technology became the norm. Polaroid ended up bankrupt. If you had decided to buy Polaroid in the 1960s and placed *all* of your portfolio in that single stock, you would have been pleased over the following 25 years. However, with digital advances, your stock would have ended up losing value.

This demonstrates the importance of diversification. Just as you might have considered the blacksmith business essential in 1900, by 1906 that business was in trouble. The automobile was new, widely available technology. We cannot know today what revolutionary changes in the future will make today's indispensable products obsolete. So for those investors who want to place capital in high-demand products, diversification (among stocks) and allocation (in dissimilar sectors) represent smart long-term management.

Creating the Winning Portfolio

What do you want to achieve in your portfolio? If you have been investing money for several years and have come through the volatile and expensive lessons of late 1990s and early 2000s, you know that there are many unseen risks, especially in the equity markets. Some people have tried to accumulate wealth quickly, not realizing the degree of risk to which they were exposed. Others, overly conservative even today, have overlooked the dangers of diminishing spending power on an after-tax and after-inflation basis.

A critical analysis of your overall goal probably will reveal that you seek the following:

- return on investment at or above the break-even point when considering both inflation and taxes

- acceptable risk based on time horizon and type of specific goal

- the ability to manage assets so that changed markets and personal circumstances do not make the portfolio obsolete

- effective methods of allocating assets based on goals and risk tolerance, but recognizing the ongoing need to modify allocation as personal situations change

- identification of *all* forms of risk and identification of steps to be taken to mitigate those risks (including diversification, movement and reallocation of funds, use of put options for insurance, and identification of alternative markets)

The winning portfolio is not going to be one that produces profits 100% of the time, nor one that provides profits rapidly. The necessary balance between risk and reward mandates a moderate approach, patience, and a willingness to accept a specific risk level in order to achieve a better *average* outcome. Asset allocation can be thought of as a guidance system for your portfolio. It is based on well-defined goals, matched with specific risk tolerance, and organized with your timeline in mind. Within an allocated portion of your portfolio, you employ diversification as a means of monitoring risk, while avoiding the tendency to diversify so much that your overall rate of return suffers.

> **Asset allocation can be thought of as a guidance system for your portfolio. It is based on well-defined goals, matched with specific risk tolerance, and organized with your timeline in mind.**

Portfolio management is a balancing act in many respects, and financial planning is a process of definition, research, and action. The creation of a model that addresses all aspect of today's requirements (often called the process of "needs analysis") is a good place to start; however, also be aware that it is only a starting point. However you see financial matters today, it is sure to change in the future.

Chapter 5

REVIEW YOUR KNOWLEDGE
Simple Steps to Asset Allocation

Chapter 1

1. **Diversification on the basis of *investment goals and objectives* is:**
   a. not an appropriate alternative because goals and objectives vary too greatly
   b. not truly diversification, but is a financial planning system
   c. the most appropriate form of diversification because it includes all relevant factors
   d. the only system recommended by the SEC

2. **In an *integrated* system of planning, you should take into account:**
   a. your goals and objectives
   b. risk tolerance
   c. appropriate levels of diversification and specific product selections
   d. all of the above

3. **Your financial plan is *dynamic* because it is affected by:**
   a. changes in markets and products, your income and capital resources, family status, job and career, and personal development
   b. movement in the Dow Jones Industrial Averages, the Consumer Price Index (CPI), and other economic forces

    c. ever-changing competitive position of companies in the same market sector

    d. political control in federal and state governments and, to a degree, changes in world political conditions

4. **When it comes to risk, remember that:**
   a. there are no foolproof plans
   b. the best investments are risk-proof, but harder to find
   c. only experts understand its complexity
   d. you can tolerate more risk as you get older

5. **Excessive diversification means:**
   a. you change your mind too often and end up churning your account
   b. you attempt to spread risk too much, resulting in lower than acceptable overall returns
   c. market conditions require placing most capital in fast-rising stocks
   d. profits are high, but your taxes absorb most of it

6. **For the purpose of analysis, your "break-even point" is:**
   a. simply the return of the capital you originally invested, plus inflation
   b. your after-tax profit from investments
   c. your return after considering the effect of both taxes and inflation
   d. your return at the point you reach your pre-set investment goals, plus tax liability, less inflation

7. **To compute your break-even point:**
   a. multiply your percentage of return by your effective tax rate
   b. divide your effective tax rate by the net of your dollar amount return less inflation loss
   c. divide your effective tax rate by the percentage return net of inflation
   d. divide your assumed rate of inflation by your percentage of after-tax income

8. **The inexperienced investor makes a mistake when he or she develops a plan for approaching the market, and then does not alter the plan when circumstances require it. The essential policy you need to bring into portfolio management involves three phases:**
   a. save, invest, cash out
   b. allocate, revise, diversify
   c. diversify, review, diversify again
   d. define, allocate, change

9. **When you invest all of your capital into a single industry, it is an example of:**
   a. failure to diversify
   b. taking advantage of short-term price rise opportunity
   c. singular industry allocation (SIA), a recognized allocation technique
   d. acceptable diversification, as long as you own three or more stocks within that industry

10. **Timing problems refer to:**
    a. problems associated with placing orders too close to each day's ending bell
    b. buying at market high and selling at market low levels
    c. placing too much capital in illiquid accounts
    d. the urgency of time remaining until retirement and how that affects today's investment allocation decisions

Chapter 2

11. **The over-diversified financial plan:**
    a. typically is designed in an attempt to remove as much risk as possible
    b. creates a situation in which opportunity for profit can be taken by only a portion of the larger portfolio
    c. may lead to a lackluster performance record
    d. all of the above

12. **An examination underlying the decisions you make in your portfolio should include questions of why:**
    a. your stocks are losing instead of making money
    b. you selected stocks as an appropriate venue
    c. the stock market has so much uncertainty
    d. supply and demand creates such uncertainty

13. **The stock market's conditions and how they change demonstrate the fact that:**
    a. any market is going to be in a constant state of change
    b. stocks are simply too risky for most people, no matter what conditions prevail
    c. even mutual fund managers cannot promise better than average performance
    d. asset allocation simply doesn't work in this particular market

14. **The amount of change you can tolerate is dependent upon:**
    a. your goals and objectives
    b. your risk tolerance level
    c. your experience and sophistication as an investor
    d. all of the above

15. **Risk tolerance levels:**
    a. must never be adjusted, because this is the key to market discipline
    b. are set by consultation between your financial and tax advisors
    c. should be adjusted as part of your asset allocation plan, and probably will need to be adjusted many times throughout your lifetime
    d. are attributes for speculators only, and do not affect conservative investors

16. **Spreading resources among various and different forms of investment is:**
    a. only a starting point in a program of asset allocation
    b. the cause of disaster in many a well-intended portfolio

c. usually counter-productive because real profits require focused planning

d. an over-rated market technique

17. **When experts announce percentages that should be allocated among various sectors, that is:**

a. the signal astute investors wait upon before they act

b. usually the result of careful study and analysis, and the advice should be heeded

c. of no use, because you are different from anyone else in terms of your goals and objectives, risk tolerance, and experience

d. forbidden under the new federal laws

18. **Your financial plan should serve as:**

a. a series of general rules, but subject to the guidance of experts for asset allocation decisions

b. the source for guidance, and that has to be based on definition, analysis, and decisions, not on any simple formula

c. the last word in how you will invest for the rest of your life

d. a written format by which you ensure that you will meet all of your personal and financial goals and objectives

19. **The problem with the usual method of calculating market volatility is:**

a. it fails to distinguish between rising and falling trading range trends and does not identify upward or downward price spikes which are untypical of the trading range

b. the 52-week formula includes recent pricing trends as well as outdated price trends (a full year ago)

c. the picture may be distorted by earnings reports and other news during the full year

d. all of the above

20. "Fundamental" volatility is:

a. the volatility in financial data rather than in price

b. the same as implied volatility

c. that portion of volatility affected *only* by market conditions and not by non-market factors

d. the longer-term trading range when exceptional price spikes have been removed from the analysis

21. "Cooking the books" refers to the practice of:

a. fixing "raw" data that has not yet been classified properly (thus "cooking" is the way that raw data is properly reported)

b. adjustments meant to improve reported results, achieved through techniques such as the use of off-balance sheet transactions, deferring or capitalizing expenses, booking revenue too early

c. negotiating mergers and acquisitions, so called because as financial reports are studied, the negotiations (and related market prices) tend to heat up

d. talking up a company's prospects to run up the stock price, also known as the "pump and dump" technique

22. Sarbanes-Oxley is:

a. the generalized rules and regulations governing the market, named after the first two SEC chairmen, Andrew Sarbanes and Robert Oxley

b. a new law banning analysts from making recommendations on television without prior approval from the Securities and Exchange Commission

c. a reference to stock market swindles, so named after the infamous 19th-century con artists who developed and used the pigeon drop to rob unsuspecting people

d. a new law instituting reforms in reporting and disclosure requirements

Chapter 3

23. The "100 years less your age" model of asset allocation is:

- **a.** a complex formula in which your age is used as a multiplier to exponentially increase the goal for overall portfolio value
- **b.** a simplified method for allocating a portfolio in percentages equal to your age, assuming you will live to the age of 100
- **c.** a calculation for internal rate of return based on the assumption that the inverse of your age should be equal to the long-term compound rate you earn on investments over your life expectancy
- **d.** none of the above

24. The concept of risk tolerance usually compares risk levels with:

- **a.** the potential profit associated with varying levels of risk
- **b.** market factors, which has as much to do with risk tolerance as your own goals
- **c.** whether we are in a bull or a bear market, since "risk" is defined differently in each
- **d.** risk acceptance, your willingness to live with risk (as opposed to what you can afford)

Chapter 4

25. Among the most persistent myths of the market is the idea that:

- **a.** it is possible for the individual to beat the odds
- **b.** investors can diversify without using a mutual fund
- **c.** there is some formula for beating the odds to get rich without working at it
- **d.** you can be a successful investor without paying for institutional research

ANSWERS

Chapter 1

1. **Diversification on the basis of** *investment goals and objectives* **is:**
   c. the most appropriate form of diversification because it includes all relevant factors

2. **In an** *integrated* **system of planning, you should take into account:**
   d. all of the above

3. **Your financial plan is** *dynamic* **because it is affected by:**
   a. changes in markets and products, your income and capital resources, family status, job and career, and personal development

4. **When it comes to risk, remember that:**
   a. there are no foolproof plans

5. **Excessive diversification means:**
   b. you attempt to spread risk too much, resulting in lower than acceptable overall returns

6. **For the purpose of analysis, your "break-even point" is:**
   c. your return after considering the effect of both taxes and inflation

7. **To compute your break-even point:**
   d. divide your assumed rate of inflation by your percentage of after-tax income

8. **The inexperienced investor makes a mistake when he or she develops a plan for approaching the market, and then does not alter the plan when circumstances require it. The essential policy you need to bring into portfolio management involves three phases:**
   d. define, allocate, change

9. **When you invest all of your capital into a single industry, it is an example of:**
   a. failure to diversify

10. **Timing problems refer to:**
    b. buying at market high and selling at market low levels

Chapter 2

11. **The over-diversified financial plan:**
    d. all of the above

12. **An examination underlying the decisions you make in your portfolio should include questions of why:**
    b. you selected stocks as an appropriate venue

13. **The stock market's conditions and how they change demonstrate the fact that:**
    a. any market is going to be in a constant state of change

14. **The amount of change you can tolerate is dependent upon:**
    d. all of the above

15. **Risk tolerance levels:**
    c. should be adjusted as part of your asset allocation plan, and probably will need to be adjusted many times throughout your lifetime

16. **Spreading resources among various and different forms of investment is:**
    a. only a starting point in a program of asset allocation

17. **When experts announce percentages that should be allocated among various sectors, that is:**
    c. of no use, because you are different from anyone else in terms of your goals and objectives, risk tolerance, and experience

18. **Your financial plan should serve as:**
    b. the source for guidance, and that has to be based on definition, analysis, and decisions, not on any simple formula

19. The problem with the usual method of calculating market volatility is:

   d. all of the above

20. "Fundamental" volatility is:

   a. the volatility in financial data rather than in price

21. "Cooking the books" refers to the practice of:

   b. adjustments meant to improve reported results, achieved through techniques such as the use of off-balance sheet transactions, deferring or capitalizing expenses, booking revenue too early

22. Sarbanes-Oxley is:

   d. a new law instituting reforms in reporting and disclosure requirements

Chapter 3

23. The "100 years less your age" model of asset allocation is:

   b. a simplified method for allocating a portfolio in percentages equal to your age, assuming you will live to the age of 100

24. The concept of risk tolerance usually compares risk levels with:

   a. the potential profit associated with varying levels of risk

Chapter 4

25. Among the most persistent myths of the market is the idea that:

   c. there is some formula for beating the odds to get rich without working at it

Resource
Guide

RECOMMENDED READING

Wealth Management

By Harold Evensky

Evensky's program places goal achievement over investment performance. The result is a wealth management program dedicated to the client, instead of the investment.

$55.00   Item #T185X-3552

Global Asset Allocation

By Wolfgang Drobetz, Peter Oertmann, and Heinz Zimmermann

Global Asset Allocation investigates whether global sector diversification strategies produce risk-return patterns different from asset allocation rules defined in terms of national markets and how the Black-Litterman model can be used to improve global asset allocation decisions.

$69.95   Item #T185X-626278

Getting Started in Asset Allocation

By Bill Bresnan and Eric Gelb

Covering the basics of starting an asset allocation program, *Getting Started in Asset Allocation* offers sound advice, helpful tips, and practical guidelines—all corresponding to your particular financial situation, whether you're single, married with children, saving for college, or retired.

$24.95   Item #T185X-10517

The Intelligent Asset Allocator

By William Bernstein

Safe, simple, PROVEN, and time-tested techniques for building your own, balanced and diversified investment portfolio. "This is a GREAT book," says John Bogle, "Any reader who takes the time and effort to understand his approach will surely be rewarded."

$29.95   Item #T185X-11574

Asset Allocation: Balancing Financial Risk

By Roger C. Gibson

Now in its third edition, the bestselling reference book on this popular subject for a decade has been updated to keep pace with the latest developments and findings. Provides step-by-step strategies for implementing asset allocation in a high return/low risk portfolio, educating financial planning clients on the logic behind asset allocation.

$55.00   Item #T185X-11021

▲ ▲ ▲ ▲ ▲ ▲

Many of these books, along with hundreds of others, are available at a discount from FP Books.
To place an order, or find out more, visit us at

www.fpbooks.com

or call us at

1-800-511-5667 ext T185

IMPORTANT WEB SITES

www.insuranceplanningadvisors.com
Halloran Financial Services, specialists in estate and financial planning, providing comprehensive solutions for insurance and long-term care needs for over 20 years. For information contact:

Halloran Financial Services
Mike@insuranceplanningadvisors.com
(781) 449-4556
400 Hillside Ave, Needham, MA 02494

www.financialpro.org
For more than 70 years, the **Society of Financial Service Professionals**—formerly the American Society of CLU & ChFC—has been helping individuals, families, and businesses achieve financial security.

www.fpanet.org
The **Financial Planning Association** is the membership organization for the financial planning community. FPA has been built around four Core Values—Competence, Integrity, Relationships and Stewardship.

www.fpbooks.com
FP Books, a division of SuperBookDeals.com, is the #1 source for financial planning and investment books, videos, software, and other related products. Find the most thorough selection of new releases and hard-to-find titles geared towards financial planners and advisors.

www.iarfc.org

The **IARFC** is the fastest growing organization in financial services, increasing nearly 3% per month—now over 2,600 professional members. Prospects and clients expect their financial advisors to maintain meaningful professional standards. There are seven hallmarks: education, examination, ethics, experience, licensing, continued conduct and continuing education.

www.bloomberg.com

Bloomberg L.P. is an information services, news and media company serving customers around the world.

www.fponline.com

Financial Planning Magazine Online is a comprehensive and searchable archive of past articles. This site also offers a number of active professional discussion rooms with subject matters ranging from financial planning to compliance.

▲ ▲ ▲ ▲ ▲ ▲

Many of these books, along with hundreds of others, are available at a discount from FP Books.
To place an order, or find out more, visit us at

www.fpbooks.com

or call us at

1-800-511-5667 ext T185

PUBLICATIONS
OF INTEREST

E-Alert
Thornburg Investment Management
www.thornburginvestments.com/

Barron's Online
www.barrons.com

The Wall Street Journal Online
http://online.wsj.com/public/us

Inside Information
Bob Veres
www.bobveres.com

Journal of Financial Planning
www.fpanet.org/journal

The Journal of Investing
www.iijoi.com

Registered Representative
www.rrmag.com

Free 2 Week Trial Offer for U.S. Residents From Investor's Business Daily:

INVESTOR'S BUSINESS DAILY will provide you with the facts, figures, and objective news analysis you need to succeed.

Investor's Business Daily is formatted for a quick and concise read to help you make informed and profitable decisions.

To take advantage of this free 2 week trial offer,
e-mail us at customerservice@fpbooks.com
or visit our website at www.fpbooks.com where you
find other free offers as well.

You can also reach us by calling 1-800-511-5667
or fax us at 410-964-0027.

About the Author

▲ ▲ ▲ ▲ ▲ ▲

MICHAEL C. THOMSETT has written over 50 finance and investment books. He is the author of the successful *Getting Started in Options* (John Wiley & Sons) now in its fifth edition, which has sold over 175,000 copies. He also wrote *Investment and Securities Dictionary*, which was named by *Choice Magazine* an outstanding academic book of the year and was also published as a Webster's Dictionary. In addition, he authored *Master Fundamental Analysis* and *Mastering Technical Analysis* (Dearborn).

Thomsett also has written several real estate investment books, including *J. K. Lasser's Real Estate Investing* (John Wiley & Sons). He resides in Washington state and has been writing for 25 years.

This book, along with other books, are available at discounts that make it realistic to provide them as gifts to your customers, clients, and staff. For more information on these long-lasting, cost-effective premiums, please call John Boyer at 800-272-2855 or e-mail him at john@fpbooks.com